Jeanloup Sieff
Dance

Jeanloup Sieff
Dance

Preface by Jeanloup Sieff

Smithsonian Institution Press
Washington, D.C.

Originally published in Italian in 1996
by Federico Motta Editore

Published 1999 in the United States of America
by Smithsonian Institution Press
in association with Federico Motta Editore, Milan

Translation from French and Italian by Renata Treitel

Library of Congress Cataloging-in-Publication Data

Sieff, Jeanloup, 1933–
   [Danza. English]
   Dance / text by Jeanloup Sieff.
      p.   cm. — (Motta fotografia)
   ISBN 1-56098-862-2 (alk. paper)
   1. Dance photography. 2. Ballet—Pictorial works. 3.
Sieff, Jeanloup, 1933– . I. Title. II. Series: Motta
fotografia (Washington, D.C.)
   TR817.5.S5413   1999
   779′.979262—dc21   98-47575

06 05 04 03 02 01 00 99   5 4 3 2 1

Printed by Arti Grafiche Motta, Milan
Manufactured in Italy, not at government expense

Dance Memories

I have always felt great tenderness for those whose bodies are the means of expression, tools, because, contrary to other artists (painters, musicians, writers . . .) their careers end at the very moment when they totally master their art. Just like top-notch athletes (tennis champions are considered *old* when they reach the age of thirty!), dancers are pushed into retirement the moment they get past the fateful age of forty and become either choreographers or teachers. That pathetic dependence on passing time has always attracted me to them because, having devoted their existence to mastery of their bodies and to plastic perfection in daily and exhausting struggles, they find themselves alone at the side of the road as soon as their bodies abandon them, when they are still in full youth.

In Lausanne, in 1953, I discovered dance and dancers. I was studying at a nearby school of photography in Vevey for a few months and was becoming silently bored, eating apple turnovers and boating on Lake Leman. Thus I fattened the swans and looked forward without impatience to the end of my adolescence, which I felt approaching.

By chance, in school, someone proposed the theme of the dance, and I discovered the long muscles, the smell of sweat, the hiss of ballet slippers on the floor, and the long, fragile necks supporting small heads with pulled-back hair. In each dancer I found again my ideal woman, very elongated, very slim, and many years later I fell in love with a sculpture by Giacometti, which summed them all up, to console myself perhaps for never having seen again the blond, spindly student whom I photographed at Boris Kniaseff's in Lausanne. Today she must be a mature woman about my age, but I find her again in each, or almost each, dancer, and her life stopped for me at that image I took in 1953, which conserves forever her youth as well as her hopes.

To say that my love for dance is a desperate quest for that silhouette glimpsed when I was twenty might be an exaggeration, but my quest must be part of that eternal search for *temps perdu,* which is typical of all existence. My own little *madeleine* is a dancer!

Therefore, in 1960, when I was invited to illustrate a book on ballet, I saw in that request a sign of fate and accepted with enthusiasm. That book was terrible—centered images, bad printing—but I was able to meet again and to photograph the living gods of my Olympus, from Nureyev to Hightower, from Claire Motte to Nina Vyroubova. Rudolf Nureyev had just escaped to the West, jumping over the barriers at Orly airport, leaving behind his past, his friends at the Kirov, and his mother, whom he would never see again. He lived in the home of a friend of mine, and I was able to attend his classes at the Theater of the Champs-Elysées where he worked with Claire Motte, the new star dancer of the Paris Opera Ballet. Today they have both disappeared, whereas at the time they symbolized youth and strength.

But, more than the gods at their practice, whatever their talent and virtues, I preferred the impersonality of the angels, who were all female for me. Male dancers frequently have large-muscled thighs and rather heavy, firm buttocks. Although that is plastically satisfying, I prefer the emotion elicited by the apparent fragility of some female dancers. On the other hand, both male and female dancers have a great advantage compared with common mortals: the intelligence of the body. Even mediocre dancers—and they do exist—become intelligent when they begin to move to fill space.

I prefer to photograph not the performance as such, where everything is weightless, easy, mastered over, but the daily, exhausting routine during which an endless fight begins again against the restive bodies that little by little submit to the will and thus become beautiful through their painful conquest of space. There is sour sweat, like the one that Churchill promised the English, even though it was diluted by tears, and the noble, cleansing sweat experienced by dancers. A dancer's sweat exalts more than it taints.

Essentially, my love for the dance comes out of the need that all unbelievers have to purify themselves by contact with the faithful. In 1974 I photographed Carolyn Carlson for the magazine *Réalités.* Because we liked each other, she invited me to work with her at the Paris Opera, where she was directing a workshop of contemporary dance. She frequently came to my studio with her dancers. Subsequently, my images were projected onto the stage of the opera during her ballet as counterpoint to her choreography.

Carolyn Carlson is like a sculpture by Giacometti to which the muse Terpsichore has given life. Her long-limbed body never stops ascending all the way to a small head with hollow cheeks and fast eyes that see everything. She could have played Death in a film by Bergman, but a tempting Death, who would have had only consenting victims. Like all great artists, she demands nothing of her dancers that she cannot do herself, and do even better. I remember a class she was giving at the Paris Opera during which her exhausted dancers could not follow what she was doing with a smile. My work with her was that of a clumsy witness trying to make his awkward presence forgotten so that he could attempt to seize a few moments that are so difficult to capture in photographs. Her presence is inexpressible. The way her body, so slender, succeeds in filling and creating space with such intensity has always amazed me. We worked together again in 1981 for a show in Paris that I dedicated to her.

After that, my contacts with dance became less frequent. Sometimes, in brief reunions, I took a picture for a magazine: Zizi Jeanmaire, Patrick Dupond, or Maurice Béjart, with whom I had an interesting conversation about being photogenic. I told him, in answer to his question, that being photogenic and being beautiful do not necessarily go together. For me, photogenic persons are *inhabited,* whereas those who are not are *empty.* He replied, "I agree with you, but you forget one essential point: the desire to give. On some evenings when the audience was not good, we danced less well, whereas we went beyond ourselves if we felt rapport and comprehension. Being photogenic is similar. One becomes more photogenic when one has the desire to give."

In 1988 I rediscovered my first memories of the Paris Opera when someone asked me to participate in a joint effort to finance the library. After photographing some corridors and some empty halls, I wrote this text, which I titled "The Phantoms of the Opera":

Because it is the nature of phantoms to be invisible, do not look for signs of their presence in these images. They were not there. On the other hand, I never ceased during those wandering days to feel their presence by my side. They have guided me inside the maze of empty corridors, up improbable stairs leading nowhere or stopped by a boarded-up door, in that tangle of narrow passages with weathered walls that hundreds of dancers have traveled up and down, their hearts pounding before they entered the immense nave of the stage.

Entire lives were devoted to those journeys of initiation with stages as immutable as the stations of the cross. After entering the ballet school at the age of nine, their young necks already crowned by a small, tight chignon, those dancers, with their firm bodies, spent all of their days there, trapped in the lights that freed them from the brittle chrysalis of the *petit rat* to the hoped-for emergence of the star dancer, an ephemeral and glorious butterfly released from gravity.

Then they vanished into the shadows of the odors of dust and wax, leaving the dream of hope to those who flocked together for an uncertain succession, an endless stream of small, straight heads stylized by the chignon, long legs that could endure pain, and children's sweat often diluted by the tears of failure.

They were all around me in those deserted corridors, in those empty studios with floorboards that remembered and that I trampled with an untutored and iconoclastic foot. I heard them whisper in the silence; here in these same places they dreamed, suffered, then cheered up, giggling in the white flight of their crisp tutus, the lesson over. Alone, in the silence that precedes or follows combat, like an unbeliever lost in a cathedral temporarily bereft of its faithful but still full of the divine presence, I remembered Cocteau, and in looking at the silence, I could hear the light.

Twenty-eight years have passed since I worked on my first book, *Le Ballet*, pacing up and down those floors in the company of dancers who are now all gone. The *phantoms of the Opera* are those of my own youth: Yvette Chaviré, Claire Motte, Liane Daydé, Serge Lifar, Youli Algaroff, Serge Golovine. . . . What has become of those anonymous dancers whom I photographed in 1960 on these empty stairs that I climbed today? What will become of these young dancers, with their serious eyes, whom I just passed in the hall? For those dancers, whose bodies are tools, the years go by quickly, very quickly, and the applause echoes still even if their presence is no more than a memory.

However, as long as a young girl is putting on her first tutu, those phantoms will live in the memory that the generations pass on to convince themselves that only what is ephemeral of Art is immortal.

Yet, my connections with dance are only nostalgic, even though each picture tells me that nothing will return. What I love in the dancers, beyond their energy and their courage, is that wonderful narcissism of theirs, which is only bearable because it is necessary, among themselves.

Besides his artistic qualities, which are immense, I love the humor of Patrick Dupond, one of those rare dancers who laughs at himself. Thus he consented to pose, naked, wearing my daughter's dancing shoes.

Marie-Claude Pietragalla, recent star of the Paris Opera Ballet, combines a devouring energy and passion with a tenderness and a curiosity for others that are very rare.

Sylvie Guillem, who has left the Paris Opera Ballet for an international career, is a unique performer, perhaps the last diva of the dance, whom imbeciles reproach for having a personality, when it is an indispensable quality.

Many are the ones I have not photographed, like Jean Babylé, who put his mark on an era and still has the silhouette of a young man, even though he is past his seventies.

Zizi Jeanmaire: the memory of her laughter and her legs will stay with me always. Roland Petit still has the curiosity and the enthusiasm of his twenties and directs the National Ballet of Marseilles.

In short, dance is a marvelous school of life because of its strictness. It is an opening on the artistic world because of its multiple exchanges with other disciplines. And it is a school of humility because of its dependence on the fragility of the bodies that express it.

Among the models I photograph for the fashion magazines, I recognize immediately the ones who have studied dance. They know how to carry their heads; they have a certain way of sitting and a natural elegance that the mastery of their bodies has shaped forever. Always with these models I take my best images because dance has given them the body intelligence that cats and gazelles possess innately.

Jeanloup Sieff

Photographs

2

4

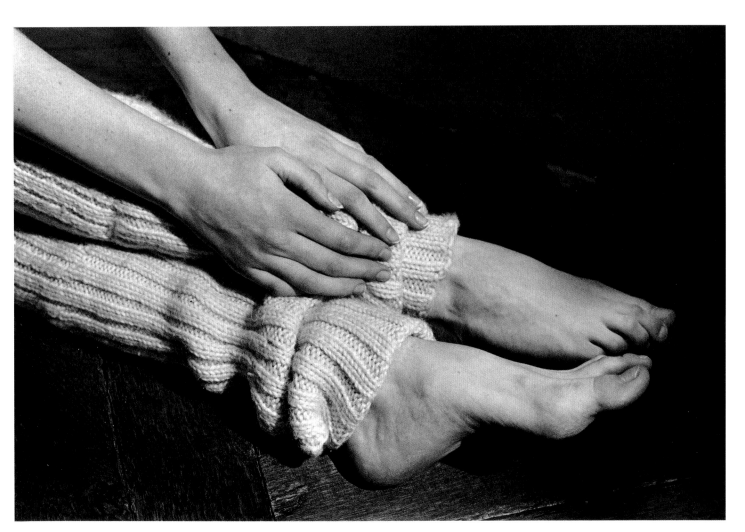

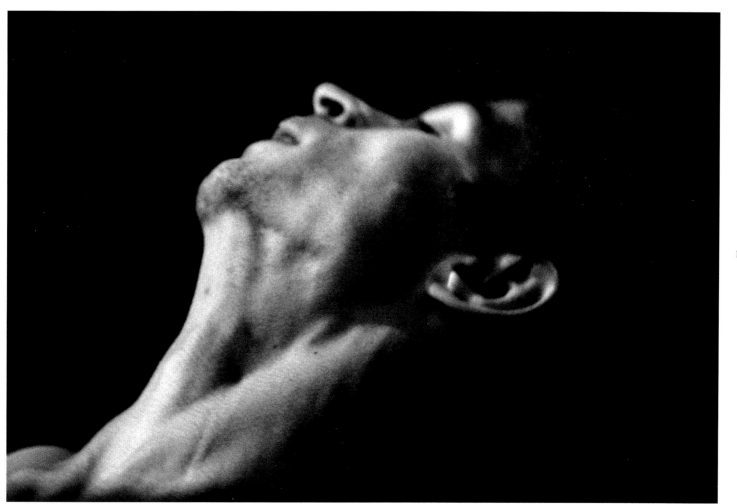

13

16

30

36